MARTIN LEMAN'S
Needlepoint Cats

NEEDLEPOINT DESIGNS BY JILL LEMAN
FROM PAINTINGS BY MARTIN LEMAN

GUILD PUBLISHING

LONDON · NEW YORK · SYDNEY · TORONTO

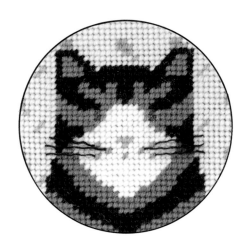

This edition published 1990 by Guild Publishing by arrangement with PELHAM BOOKS

Copyright © Jill and Martin Leman, 1990

Typeset in Garamond ITC Book by Goodfellow and Egan, Cambridge

Colour reproduction by Anglia Graphics, Bedford

Printed and bound by Times Publishing Group Ltd, Singapore

A CIP catalogue record for this book is available from the British Library.

CN 5603

Contents

Before you start

For those who are new to needlepoint/canvas work there are a few basic things you should know before you begin sewing.

CANVAS

There are two kinds of canvas you can use to make the cat designs in this book. They are single thread canvas (sometimes called mono) and double thread canvas (sometimes called Penelope). Single canvas is available in various sizes. The sizes I use in this book are 14 and 10 holes to the inch. It is stiffer than double canvas and should be worked in tent stitch, with yarn appropriate to the size of the mesh.

Double canvas has two threads running in each direction and is essential if you work in half cross stitch. An advantage of double canvas is that you can push the threads apart to be evenly spaced and work this area in stitches half the size of the surround called 'petit point'. This can be useful for details such as a cat's eyes and nose. Double canvas is normally to be found with 10 holes to the inch.

Work the canvas with the selvedge vertical, leaving about two inches all around the area of the needlepoint so that you have some space to use when you come to stretching and mounting the finished work. It is a good idea to tape over all the edges of the canvas with masking tape so that when you are sewing the yarn does not catch on the canvas edge and fray.

NEEDLES

Tapestry needles are blunt and have a long eye to accommodate the yarn you are using. To sew the designs in this book I used needle size no.20 and no.18.

SCISSORS

You will need a small pair of sharp clean scissors.

YARNS

The yarns used to work the designs in this book are Paterna Persian, Anchor Tapisserie or DMC. Paterna has three strands of yarn loosely twisted together. This enables you to divide the strands easily and use one, two, three or more in the needle depending on the canvas you are using. You can also mix colours by using one or more strands of each colour in the needle.

Anchor Tapisserie and DMC are called tapestry wools and are not stranded.

All three brands of yarn are available at specialist shops throughout the UK but should you have any difficulty in obtaining what you need, you can write to the manufacturers. You will find their addresses at the end of this book.

COLOUR AND MAKE OF YARN

The colour and make of yarn for each design in this book is listed with the charted designs. If your local supplier has different yarns or a narrower choice of colours I suggest you take this book to the shop and, using the colour reproduction of the finished needlepoint as a guide, choose your own range. If this is not possible the list of stockists at the back of this book will provide you with mail order addresses.

AMOUNT OF YARN

The amount of yarn needed for each design in this book has been specified as closely as possible. It is difficult to be absolutely accurate because depending on which sort of canvas used, on what size and which stitch, the amount of yarn needed can vary considerably.

STITCHES

You need to know how to do the following stitches:

Tent stitch – this can be used on both single and double canvas. It is a hard-wearing stitch but uses up more yarn than half cross stitch.

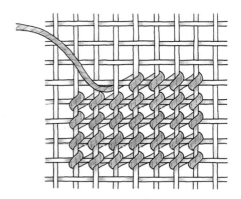

Bring needle out and take it up to right over one canvas intersection. Insert downwards under 2 vertical threads and 1 horizontal one. Bring needle out ready to form next stitch. On subsequent rows work into the heads of the stitches in the previous rows. The back of the work is made up of long diagonal stitches all slanting the same way.

Half cross stitch – this should only be used on double canvas. It is not used on single canvas because it doesn't cover the canvas threads sufficiently.

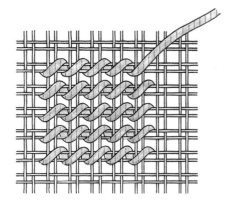

This has the appearance of tent stitch but is worked differently. Starting at left, bring needle out and take it up to right over 1 canvas intersection. Insert downwards under one horizontal double thread and bring needle out ready to form next stitch. The back of the work is made up of short vertical stitches.

Cross stitch – this can be useful for cats' eyes and noses where more emphasis is needed.

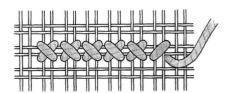

Bring needle out at left and take it up to right over 1 canvas intersection. Insert needle downwards under 1 horizontal thread. Take needle up to left over stitch just formed and insert down to bring out in same spot to make next stitch.

Random long and short stitch – this is worked on single canvas in this book. It gives a very fur-like texture and is quicker to work than either tent stitch or half cross stitch. Stitches can be made over two, three, four, five or six threads but should be staggered, to give an even all-over texture.

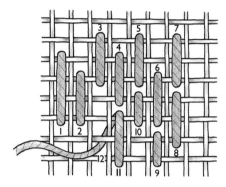

Work in varying lengths along each row from left to right, then work the following row right to left.

WORKING FROM THE CHARTS

It is very simple to work from the charted designs in this book. On the charts, each square represents one stitch on your canvas. The size of canvas you decide to use does not make any difference – whether it is double mesh with 10 holes to the inch or single mesh with 14 holes to the inch – one square on the chart will still equal one stitch on the canvas. To make the charts easy to follow, I have used coloured dots to show the number of stitches in each colour that you will be sewing. These dots are in more exaggerated colours than the yarns so that they are easier to count. Each area of colour on the charts is outlined in black to help you see exactly where

you are. You might find it helpful to mark where you are on the chart by using a ruler.

The finished needlepoints and the charts have been reproduced as large as the page size of the book allows to help you to see clearly which colours to use.

WHEN YOU SEW

Sit in a comfortable position.
Have clean hands.
Work in good light.
Have about 18″/45cm of yarn in the needle.
Try to keep your stitching even.

I don't think you should worry about the back of your needlepoint – some people are naturally neat and others are not. I feel it's more important to enjoy what you are making so that you finish the needlepoint. Once you have framed it or made it into a cushion no one will ever see the back.

The more needlepoint you do, the easier it becomes and you could always go to a class to learn how to perfect your technique.

FINISHING YOUR WORK

The needlepoints in this book were worked without a frame and tended to become distorted. I have found that single mesh canvas is more likely to lose its shape than double mesh.

To stretch or block the canvas back into shape you will need a piece of insulation board bigger than your canvas. Insulation board is easy to press drawing pins into. Cover the board with a piece of polythene, then pin a clean tea-towel or several sheets of blotting paper onto the board and dampen the tea-towel/blotting paper with clean water using a plant spray. Place the needlepoint face down on the tea-towel/blotting paper and dampen the back. Using rustless drawing pins pin out the canvas working from side to side – one pin on the left, one pin on the right. As you proceed, gently pull the canvas into shape – use a ruler and set square to check. You can dampen the work quite thoroughly as long as any marking on the canvas has been made with a waterproof pen. Do not be in too much of a hurry, it does take time and patience. When the work is straight, leave it to dry thoroughly – for at least 24 hours. If the work is very distorted you can repeat the process, but I feel that handmade objects have a certain character and that they do not have to be rigidly accurate.

PICTURES

If you would like to frame the finished work, cut a piece of mounting board (which you can get from an art supplier) to the size of the finished work. Lay the work over the board centring it carefully. Fold the edges of the canvas to the back of the board. Using strong thread, lace opposite edges to each other beginning at the centre and working out to the corners. Use close herringbone stitches and pull together the edges tightly and evenly. Check as you go that the needlepoint stays in the correct position on the board. Complete the two opposite sides before starting the other two. Finish off securely. Your work is now ready to be framed.

CUSHIONS

If the finished needlepoint is the size of the cushion you want, find a firm fabric suitable for backing. Place the needlepoint right sides together with the backing, stitch round three sides and a little round the corners of the fourth side. Turn right side out, insert a cushion pad and slipstitch. You could then add a twisted braid trim in colours that suit the needlepoint and a tassel at each corner. If the needlepoint is smaller than the cushion size you want, you can add a fabric border, and proceed as before.

For more detailed instructions there are many excellent books on soft furnishing available.

Red

$\mathcal{T}$his large stripey cat would make a rather grand cushion edged with twisted braiding and tassels.
I simplified his stripes for the needlepoint design. His eyes and nose could be worked in petit point as shown here or as the chart on the next page.
Red was worked in half cross stitch on double mesh canvas with 10 holes to the inch.

Canvas

You will need double mesh canvas with 10 holes to the inch measuring approximately 44×66cm/17½×26in. Beige or écru colour is preferable to white, if available, because any canvas threads not covered by the yarn will not show up so glaringly. Finished size of the worked needlepoint is 33×57cm/13×22½in.

Yarn

Anchor Tapisserie
(*Numbers in brackets show how many skeins of yarn you will need for each colour*)

3229	Cream for cat's fur	(6)
384	Off-white for chest and paws	(2)
0403	Black for background	(5)

Paterna Persian
Use two strands of yarn in the needle

A882	Ginger stripes, use one strand of each	
A723	colour in the needle (3 skeins of each)	
A421	Dark brown on cat's face and eyes	(1)
A801	Bright orange for eyes	(1)
D541	Eye colour	(1)
D281	Pink for nose	(1)
A660	Dark green foreground	(6)
A661	Light green for foreground highlights	(2)

Whiskers

Red's whiskers were added after the needlepoint had been stretched. Take one strand of Paterna Persian yarn (A430) about six inches long and gently untwist it. You will have a piece of slightly wavy yarn. Thread this onto a needle, tie a knot in the end and bring the needle through from the back of the needlepoint to one of the dots marking the position of the whiskers. Judge the length and position of the whisker, then take it through the needlepoint to the back and finish off securely. You will probably only be able to do one whisker at a time.

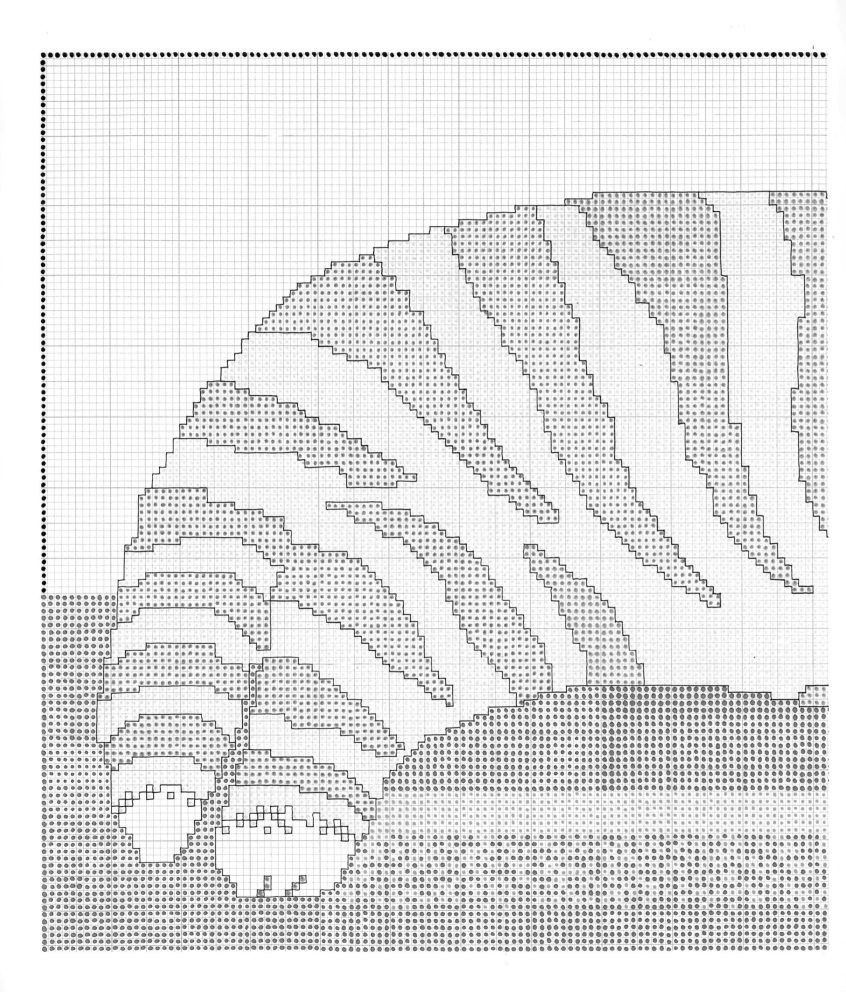

12

Boris

The original Boris was a lino-cut print in one colour. I have adapted the design to show a smart black and white cat with a spotted tie, framed by a brightly striped border. This design is quick and easy to sew in random long and short stitch for the cat, with tent stitch eyes and nose. Straight stitch is used for everything else.
As this needlepoint was designed to be framed, the straight stitches can be sewn over as many as 14 threads.

How to start

The outline shown here is the actual size to use for a finished picture. The easiest way to transfer the outline to your canvas is to first trace the outline from the book onto tracing paper using a black felt tip pen. Tape the tracing onto a window, then hold your canvas against the tracing paper. You should be able to see the outline clearly. Using a red, green or blue waterproof (very important) felt tip pen, you can now trace the design onto the canvas. Follow the photograph on the previous page for stitch details and colours. The original needlepoint has been reproduced larger than its actual size to show these clearly.

To experiment with other colours you could use colour pencils on your tracing and see which colours work together – perhaps a grey and white cat with a black background and a pink/white/blue border.

Canvas

You will need a 30cm/12in square of single mesh canvas with 14 holes to the inch.

Yarn

Anchor Tapisserie
(*Numbers in brackets show how many skeins of yarn you will need for each colour*)

0403	Black for cat's body (1)	
0402	White for face and paw (1)	
0139	Blue for background and outside border (2)	
0238	Green for tie and striped border (1)	
0748	Red for ball and border (1)	
0298	Yellow for moon, eyes, spots on tie and border (1)	
0217	Dark green for grass (1)	

Whiskers

The whiskers are worked in straight stitch using Anchor Tapisserie – see colour reproduction of Boris for details.

Tiny Tom

This little striped cat sitting on a checked floor in front of flowered wallpaper has such an appealing expression that it is hard to put him down once started.

As the design is so simple, the colours could easily be changed, perhaps to those of your own kitten.

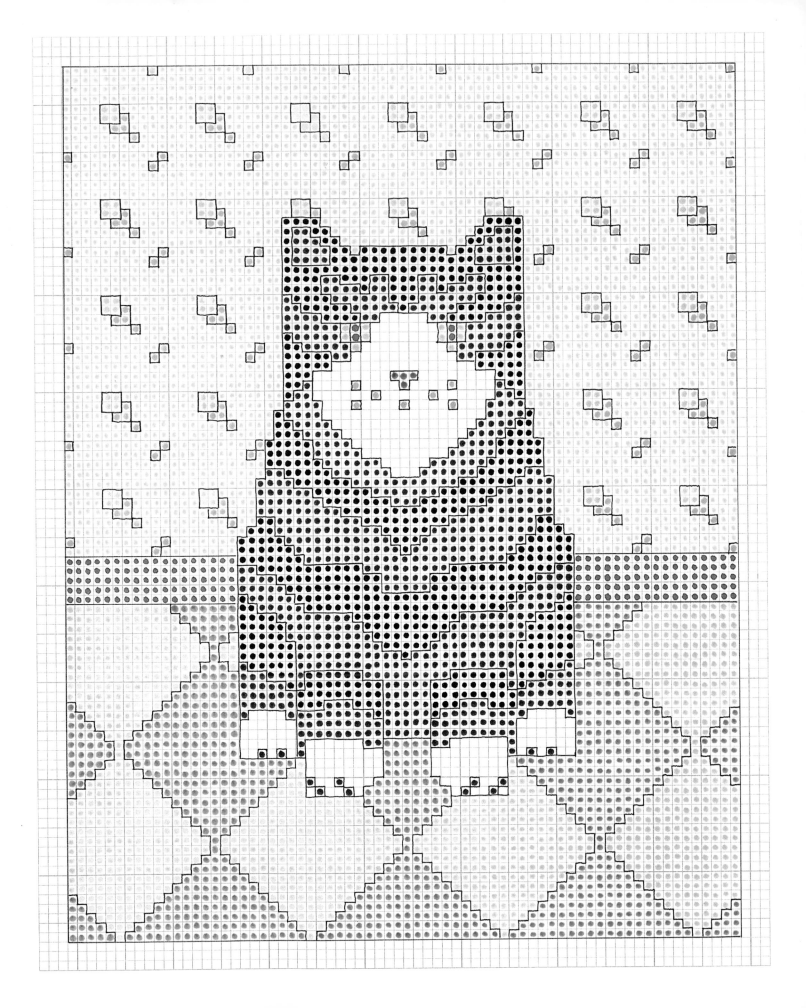

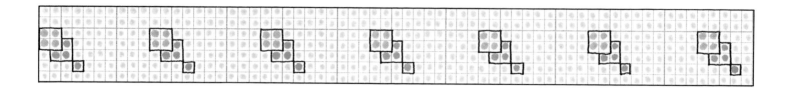

When planning the needlepoint of Tiny Tom, I thought it would be good to have a fairly simple design with areas broken up into different colours in order to keep the interest going. Enthusiasm can run out quickly when there are large areas of plain colour to cover. Tiny Tom was sewn in tent stitch on double mesh canvas and the finished needlepoint was framed.

Canvas

You will need double mesh canvas with 10 holes to the inch measuring approximately 33×28cm/ 13×11in.

If available off-white canvas is preferable to white.

Finished size of needlepoint 23.5×18cm/9⅛×7⅛in.

Yarn

DMC Tapisserie

(Numbers in brackets show how many skeins of yarn you will need for each colour)

7457	Ginger for cat (2)	
7508	Black for cat (2)	
Écru	Cat's face and paws (1)	

Anchor Tapisserie

3122	Pink for nose (1)
0373	Whiskers, spots and mouth (1)
0564	Blue for floor, wallpaper and eyes (2)
0849	Dark blue for eyes and skirting (1)
0726	Creamy yellow for floor (2)
0729	Cream for wallpaper (2)
0859	Green for wallpaper (1)

Whiskers

Follow the instructions given for the Red needlepoint.

Tibby & Scamper

The portrait Martin painted of 'Tibby & Scamper' was commissioned a few years ago by their owners. I thought it would be fun to sew a small version, and try to keep the shapes as simple as possible so that a beginner to needlepoint would be able to follow the chart easily.
The way the two cats blend into each other and yet have quite different expressions gives the design its character.

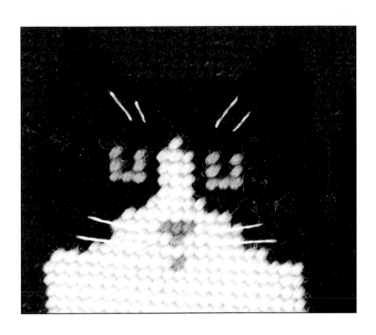

I worked the design on single mesh canvas with 14 holes to the inch, but for someone new to needlepoint it would be better to work with tent or half cross stitch on double mesh canvas with 10 holes to the inch. If you decide to do this, you will need a larger piece of canvas. You can estimate the size from the chart, which is marked in one inch squares, with ten divisions to the inch.

Canvas

You will need single mesh canvas with 14 holes to the inch measuring approximately 28×28cm/11×11in.
Finished size of needlepoint 17cm/6¾in. square.

Yarn

Anchor Tapisserie
(*Numbers in brackets show how many skeins of yarn you will need for each colour*)

0386	White for cats	(2)
0403	Black for cats	(2)
0313	Yellow for eyes	(1)
3122	Pink for noses	(1)

Paterna Persian – using two strands unless you find you get good coverage with just one strand

A900	Maroon for background	(2)
A951	Red for foreground	(1)

Whiskers

I used one strand of white cotton embroidery thread, 'Mouline Stranded'. Cut about a 12 inch length of the cotton, then separate one thread from the strand. Thread this through an embroidery needle, fasten securely at the back of the needlepoint, and following the reproduction of the needlepoint on the previous page, sew the whiskers. Fasten off securely.

Gilda

This comfortable cat curled up on a cushion is keeping an eye on her surroundings.

The stripes on the cat are more strongly defined on the needlepoint than in the painting, and I simplified the cushion by using a toning range of pinks and reds.

Gilda was worked on a large size of double mesh canvas – 7 holes to the inch, so I used two strands of tapestry wool in the needle when stitching. The finished size of the needlepoint is 32×43cm/12½×17in, which makes a good cushion size. If you use canvas with 10 or 14 holes to the inch the finished design would be smaller and could be framed as a picture.

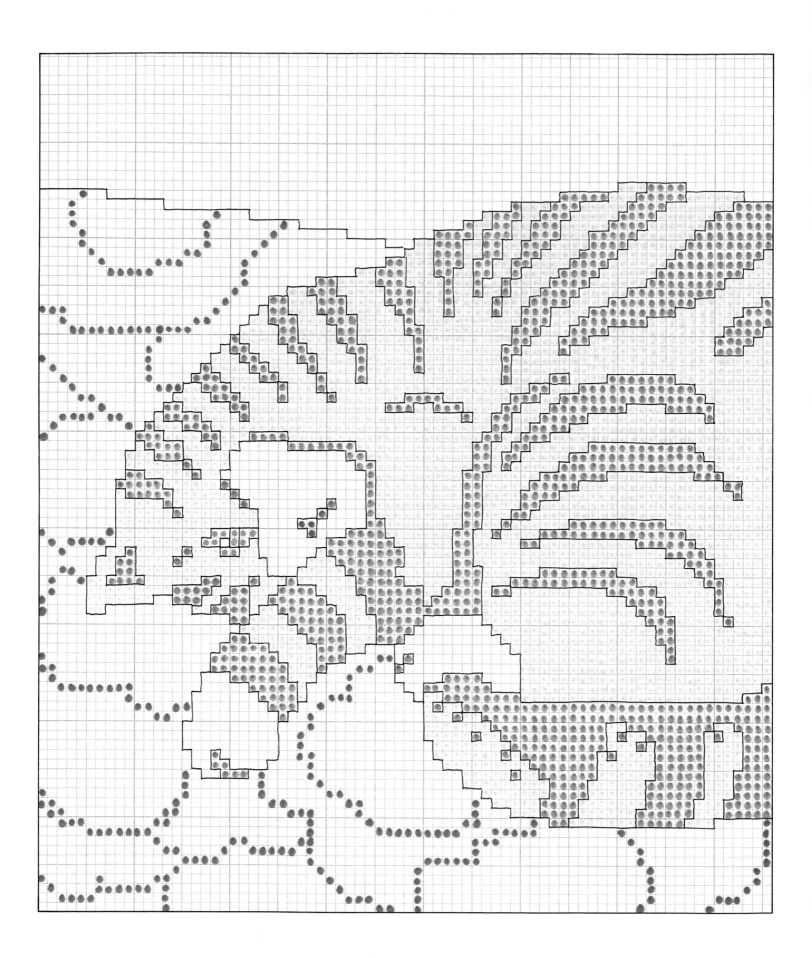

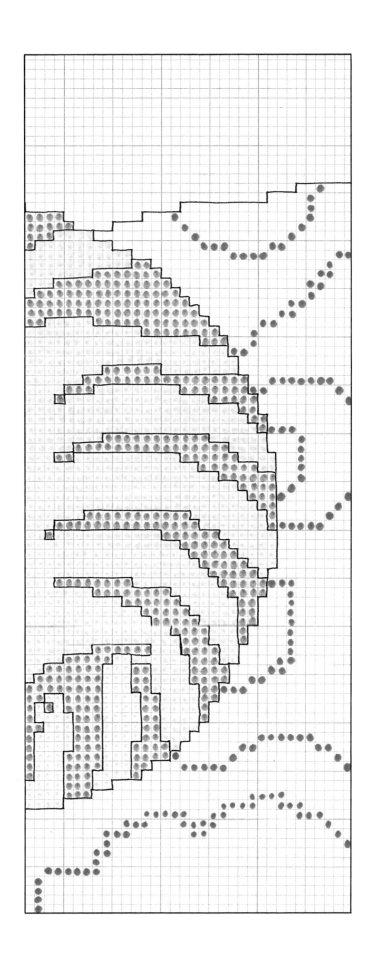

Canvas

To make the design shown on the previous page you will need double mesh canvas with 7 holes to the inch, measuring approximately 42×54cm/ 16½×21in. Finished size of worked needlepoint 32×43cm/12½×17in.

Yarn

DMC Tapisserie — using two strands of the yarn. (*Numbers in brackets show how many skeins of yarn you will need for each colour*)

7579	Cream for main body of the cat (6)	
7472	Darker cream for cat's stripes, use one	
7503	strand of each colour in needle. (2 skeins of each colour)	
Écru	Off-white for paws and face (1)	
7194	Pink for nose (1)	
7703	Green for eye (1)	
7518	Fawn for pupil (1)	
7192	Pale pink for background (3)	

For the cushion you will need about six skeins of assorted pinks and reds in dark (7199), medium (7196) and light (7194). Using the outline on the chart as a guide, and also the picture of the finished needlepoint on the previous page, fill in the floral shapes using the darkest colour at the centre and blending outwards. Do not worry if your cushion is not exactly like the photograph, enjoy making your cushion different.

Patch

When looking through a book of Martin's paintings for a cat that would make a good design for long straight stitches, I found Patch. I changed the colours slightly and added an extra patch on the cat's body

in order to break up the area of white to be covered.

I thought the finished Patch needed a friend so I did Oscar, another version, this time in grey and black. The outlines of both cats are reproduced to the size you will be sewing. All you have to do is draw around the outline in black felt tip pen on tracing paper, and transfer your tracing to the canvas by the method described for Boris on page 15.

The eyes of both cats are worked in tent stitch and the background is worked in straight rows covering four vertical threads. All the other stitches are straight, long stitches used to 'colour in' the areas you have traced onto your canvas.

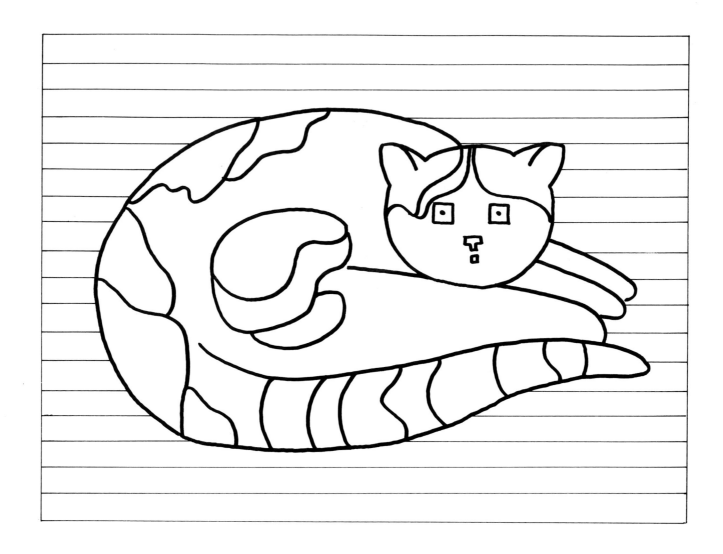

Canvas

For both cats you will need single thread canvas with 14 holes to the inch, measuring approximately 23×27cm/9×11in.
Finished size of each needlepoint 13×17.5cm/5×7in.

Yarn for Patch

DMC Tapisserie
(*You will need one skein of each colour*)

7309	Black
Blanc	White
7780	Ginger
7742	Yellow for eyes
7213	Pink for nose

Paterna Persian
Use two strands of yarn in needle
A534   Background (2)

Yarn for Oscar

DMC Tapisserie

(*You will need one skein of each colour*)

7620   Grey for cat's body

7309   Black for stripes

Blanc   White for face, paws and tip of tail

7742   Yellow for eyes

Paterna Persian

Use two strands of yarn in needle

A683   Background (2)

Whiskers

I used one strand of embroidery cotton 'Mouline Stranded' in black. Knot the thread and carefully push the needle through the canvas to where you want the first whisker to start. Then, when you have decided on the length of the whisker, push the needle through to the back ready to position the next whisker. Do this until you have six whiskers.

Home Sweet Home

This delightful cat family is worked in random long and short stitch, using tent stitch for details such as eyes, noses and inside the kitten's ears. The original oil painting was quite complex and I found that a simplified version worked better.

The outline shown on the next page is the actual size you will need to use for transferring to your canvas. The easiest way to transfer the outline is to first trace it from the book onto tracing paper using a thick black felt tip pen. Tape the tracing onto a window, then hold your canvas against the tracing paper. You should be able to see the outline clearly. Using a red, green or blue

waterproof felt tip pen, you can now trace the outline onto the canvas. It is important to use a waterproof felt tip because if you need to stretch the canvas at a later date, anything other than a waterproof pen will run. Work the tent stitch details first and then fill in with the long and short stitch. Try to keep an even overall texture.

Canvas

You will need single mesh canvas with 14 holes to the inch, measuring approximately 35×42cm/14×17in.

The finished size of the needlework is 25.5×32cm/10×12½in.

Yarn

Anchor Tapisserie

(Numbers in brackets show how many skeins of yarn you will need for each colour)

0701	Red background (2)
0217	Green foreground (2)
0359	Brown for box (2)
3122	Pale pink for blanket and noses
3166	Dark pink for blanket
0726	Cream for cat (1)
0722	Dark cream for ears
400	Dark grey for cat (1)
0398	Light grey for shading on cat, eyes and inside of kitten's ears (1)
0386	White for faces (2)
0140	Blue for eyes
0403	Black for eyes and spots on the box (1)

Whiskers

Take a 17cm/6in length of one strand of Paterna Persian yarn A202 or A261. Carefully separate and untwist the strand so that you have a length of slightly wavy yarn. Thread a needle with this and working from the front, take the needle in at one of the spots on the face and bring it out at the spot on the other side of the nose. You will now have a pair of whiskers. Trim the yarn to the length required. Then using a sharp needle and sewing cotton in grey or white, sew two or three tiny stitches over the whisker to hold it in place. Repeat on all the cats.

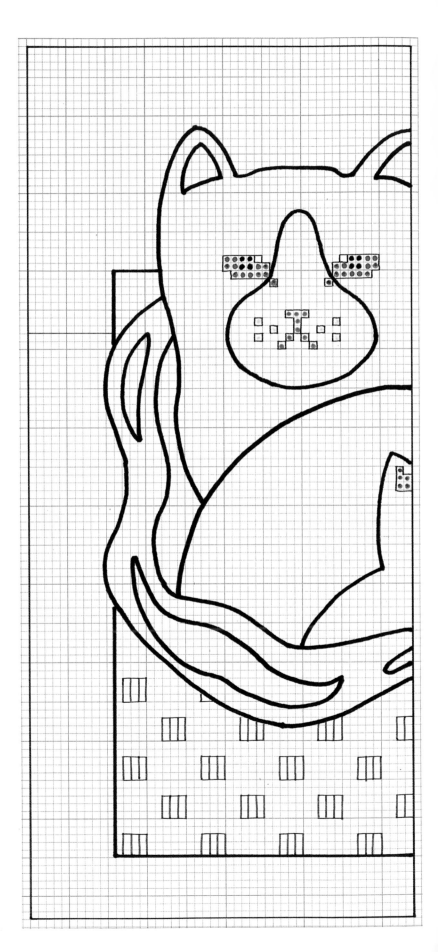

The cat in the charted design on the next page has a white chest and legs as does the original painting. The finished needlepoint shown here has a light brown chest and legs. I have given yarn amounts for both versions, so you can choose whether to follow the chart exactly or refer to the finished needlepoint. I used single mesh canvas with 10 holes to the inch as I wanted to teach myself tent stitch. In fact double mesh canvas would be better; firstly, I find it does not distort as much as single canvas on a large piece of work and secondly, it is available in a colour called 'Antique'. Using 'Antique' on this design would mean that it would not be noticeable when the yarn did not completely cover the canvas, whereas with white canvas the odd bit does show.

Canvas

You will need single or double mesh canvas with 10 holes to the inch measuring approximately 51×46cm/20×18in.
Finished size of worked needlepoint is 41×33cm/16×13in. Don't forget that if you use single mesh canvas you must sew in tent stitch.

Homeguard

Adapted from the painting 'Coastguard', this large tabby cat is intended to be made into a cushion rather than framed as a picture as I liked the idea of a life-sized needlepoint cat keeping guard from a chair at home. I felt a domestic background was therefore more in keeping and so I used a wallpaper design from another painting rather than the original seascape.

Yarn

Paterna Persian
Use two strands of yarn in the needle.
(*Numbers in brackets show how many skeins of yarn you will need for each colour*)

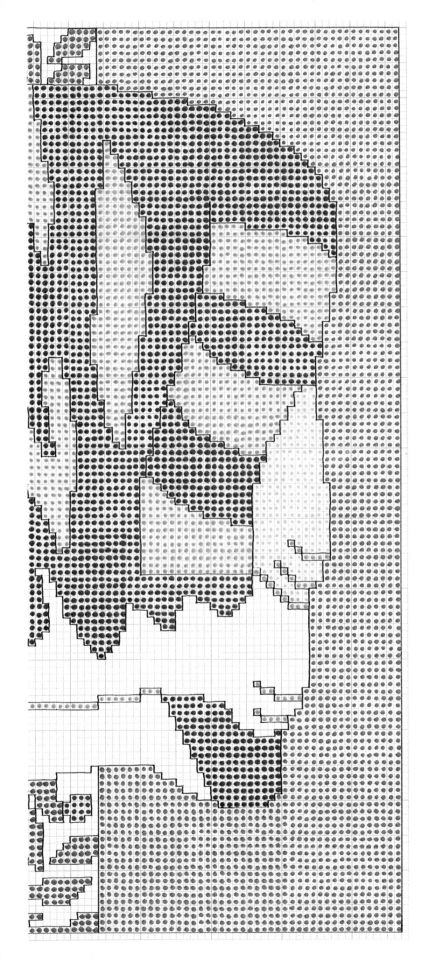

A436   Light brown for cat's face (1) or (3) if following needlepoint

A433   Mid brown for cat's markings (3)

A430   Dark brown for markings (5)

A262   Creamy white on face, chest and paws (3) or (1) if following needlepoint

A703   Yellow for eyes (1)

A710   Orange for eyes (1)

A220   Black for eyes (1)

A604   Light green for wallpaper (4)

A601   Dark green for leaves and foreground (6)

A950   Red for berries (1)

The eyes, nose and mouth are worked in cross stitch to give greater definition.

Whiskers

The whiskers were added when the needlepoint was finished by taking one strand of Paterna Persian yarn in white or light brown. If you gently untwist a short strand you will be left with a piece of slightly wavy yarn. Thread this through a needle and having secured it at the back of the needlepoint, bring it through to the front next to one of the stitches which shows the position of the whiskers. Judge the length and position of the whisker then take it through to the back and finish off. You may only be able to do one whisker at a time.

Jeffery

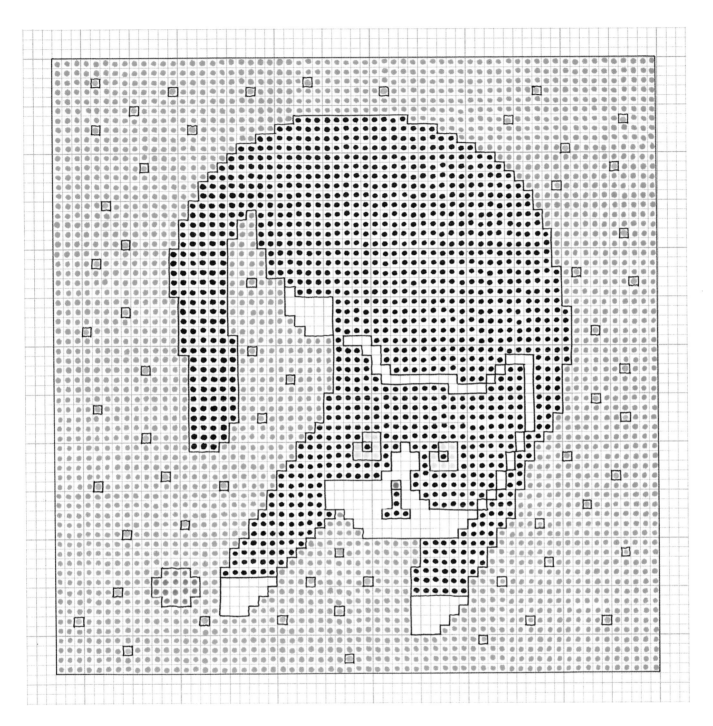

The original of Jeffery is an etching in black and white. Designing the needlepoint was an opportunity to introduce some colour into the background.
The needlepoint is sewn in half cross stitch on double mesh canvas with 10 holes to the inch.

Canvas

You will need approximately 26cm/10in square piece of double thread canvas with 10 holes to the inch. The canvas should be beige or écru in preference to white.

Finished size of needlepoint approximately 16.5cm/6½in square.

Yarn

Anchor Tapisserie

(*Numbers in brackets show how many skeins of yarn you will need for each colour*)

0403	Black for cat's body	(2)
0386	White for face and paws	(1)
0216	Green for background	(2) or
849	Blue for background (Linus)	
0068	Pink for nose and ball	(1)
0727	Yellow for eyes	(1)
0384	Cream spots on background	(1)

Whiskers

The whiskers were added after the needlepoint was finished and stretched using one strand of Paterna Persian yarn in white. Look carefully at the reproduction of the finished needlepoint for the position of the whiskers.

Linus

*W*hile I was stitching Jeffery I thought of my brother's family who own a large black and white cat called Linus. I altered the markings on the cat design accordingly and my sister-in-law stitched the portrait, this time with a blue background. These cats would be a good project for a beginner or anyone who likes to get quick results. More experienced needlepointers could have fun changing the cat's markings to create their own cat's portrait.

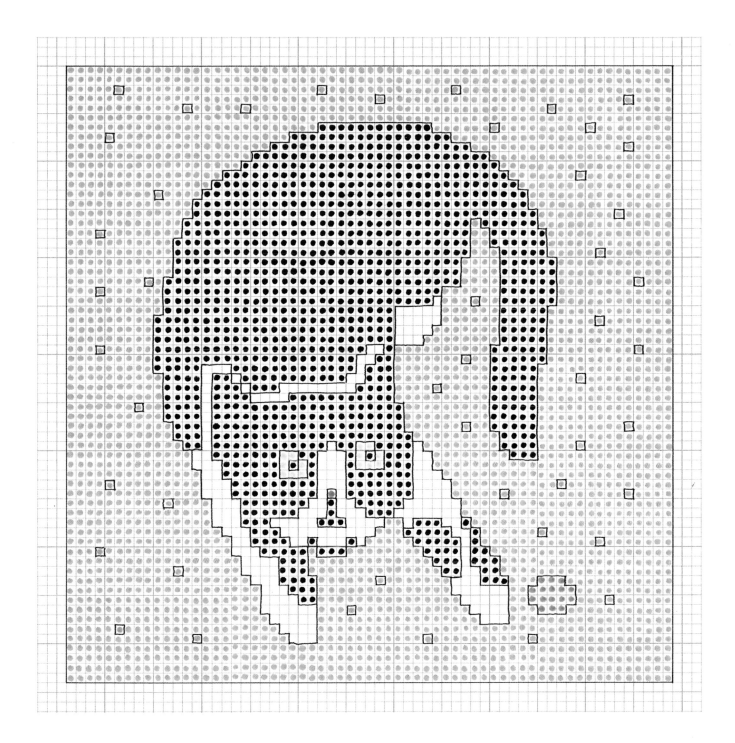

Scruffty

*O*ur Scruffty is a long-haired
tortoise-shell and white cat, and has
been the subject of several of Martin's
paintings over the years.

I have sometimes seen Victorian
woolwork pictures of cats in antique
shops, and thought how nice it would
be to have a needlepoint of Scruffty,
resplendent on a cushion, as the
Victorian cats are often shown.

As I intended this needlepoint to be
framed, I worked it on a small size
canvas.

Now that the needlepoint is finished, I would also like to see the design worked on 10 hole to the inch canvas as it would make a superb cushion, especially if trimmed with twisted braid and tassels at each corner. If your cat has tortoise-shell markings, why not adapt the design?

Canvas

You will need single mesh canvas with 14 holes to the inch, measuring approximately 26×31cm/ 10×12in.

Finished size of needlepoint approximately 18×23cm/7×9in.

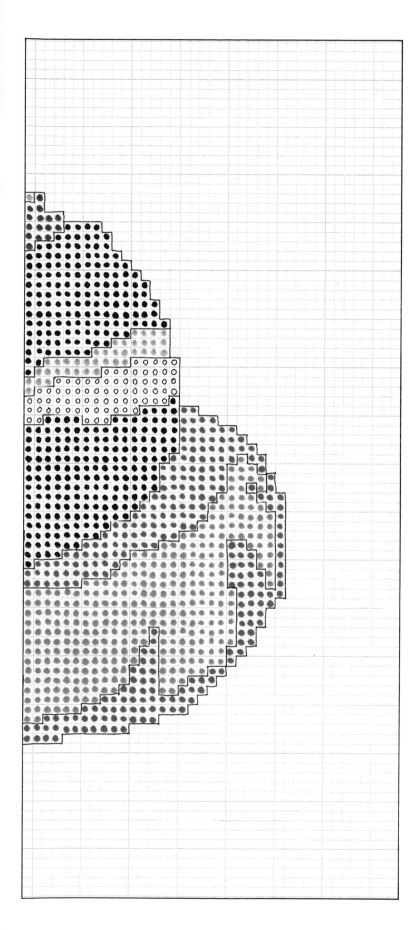

Yarn

Paterna Persian

Use two strands of yarn in the needle. You may find that you only need one strand on the lighter colours.

(*Numbers in brackets show how many skeins of yarn you will need for each colour*)

A436 Beige for cat (1)

D411 Ginger for markings (1)

A430 Dark brown for cat (1)

A420 Black for cat (1)

A261 White for cat (1)

A710 Yellow for eyes (1)

Scrap of pink for nose such as Anchor 3122

D234 Pale pink for cushion (1)

D211 Dark pink for cushion (1)

Whiskers

I used one strand of white embroidery cotton 'Mouline Stranded'. Cut about a 12in length of the cotton, then separate one thread from the strand. Thread through an embroidery needle, fasten securely at the back of the needlepoint, and following the reproduction of the needlepoint on the previous page, sew the whiskers. Fasten off securely.

Pip

This striped grey and black cat is definitely a descendant of the original 'cat sat on the mat'. My original plan was to make the needlepoint carpet exactly like the one in the painting, but the colours were so numerous that they seemed to dominate the design and finally I settled for red, green and blue stripes with a fringed border. Pip was sewn in half cross stitch on double mesh canvas.

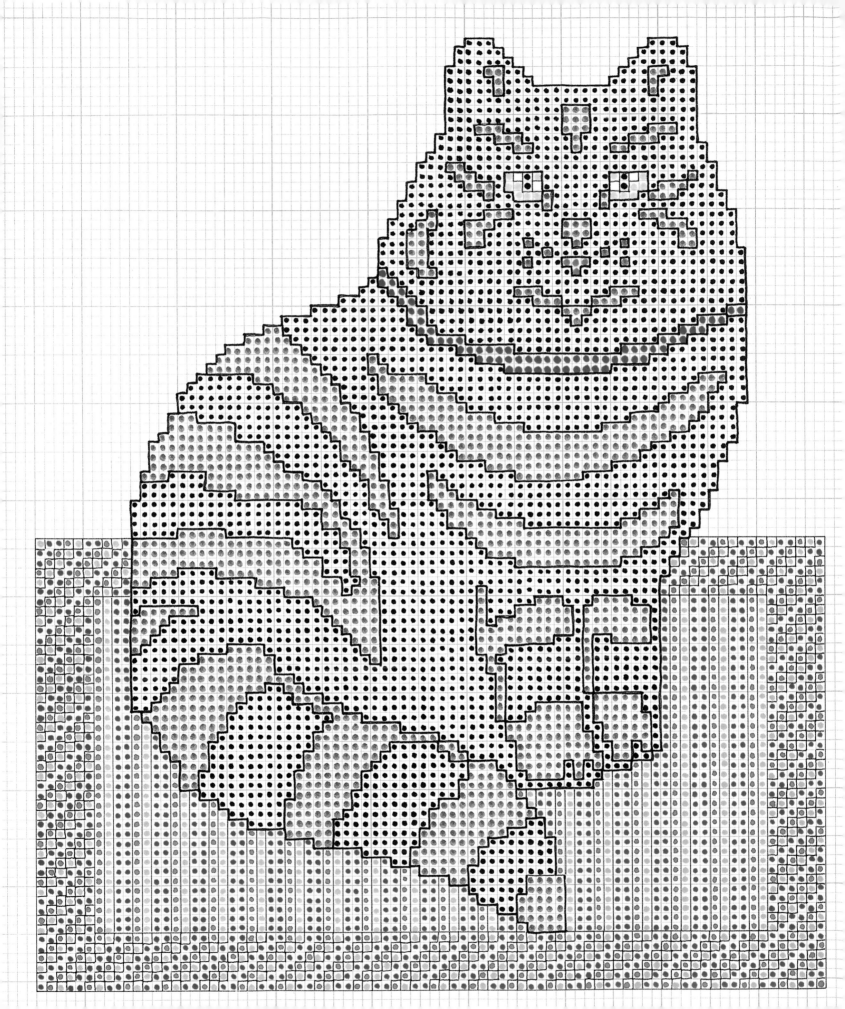

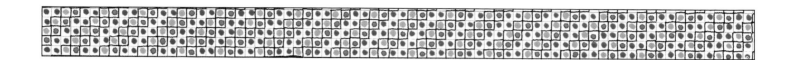

Canvas

You will need double mesh canvas with 10 holes to the inch, measuring approximately 40×36cm/16×14in. The finished size of the worked needlepoint is 32×25cm/12¾×10in.

Yarn

Anchor Tapisserie

(*Numbers in brackets show how many skeins of yarn you will need for each colour*)

0403	Black for cat's body (3)
0398	Grey for stripes (2)
0727	Yellow for eyes (1)
3122	Pink for mouth (1)
0732	Cream for background (6)
0634	Red for carpet (1)
0850	Blue for carpet (1)
0654	Green for carpet (1)

Whiskers

The whiskers were added after the needlepoint had been stretched. I used two strands of embroidery cotton 'Mouline Stranded'. Thread an embroidery needle, secure the thread at the back of the needlepoint and sew the whiskers in position, referring to the colour picture on the previous page.

Knotted Fringe

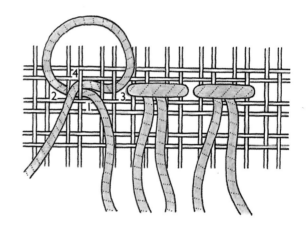

Working from left to right, insert needle at 1, leaving about an inch of yarn at the front. Bring the needle out at 2, and back in at 3, forming a loop as shown above.

Bring needle out again between two horizontal threads at 4 and pull to close loop. Trim all the ends together when the fringe is finished.

Cross Stitch Cats

The last needlepoint in this book is a little different. For all those who feel that a house is not a home without at least one cat as a resident, here is a cross stitch design.

Two cats, reminiscent of those Staffordshire pottery pairs, sit on either side of a neat house. Above the house is the alphabet and date, below the legend 'Home Sweet Home'. The picture is surrounded by a border of stylised strawberries.

The colours were chosen to give a faded, slightly antique look to the picture, but it would also look good with brighter colours – perhaps using just one colour for all the lettering. The cats could be a plain colour too, perhaps lucky black.

The picture was worked in cross stitch on écru coloured double mesh canvas with 10 holes to the inch.

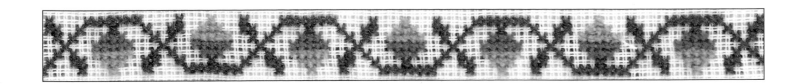

Canvas

You will need double mesh canvas with 10 holes to the inch, in écru, size approximately 40×34cm/15¾×13½in.

Finished size of cross stitch picture approximately 30×24cm/12×9½in.

Yarn

Paterna Persian

Use one strand of yarn in the needle.

(*You will need one skein of each colour.*)

D234   Dark pink for A I O T and border

D281   Pale pink for G M Y and border

A603   Pale green for B F Q U, window frames, front door

A434   Fawn for C N X, body of cats, and front path

A922   Dirty pink D K R V and house front

A503   Pale blue for E P S Z and decoration to left and right of HOME

D541   Creamy yellow H L W and cat's markings

A501   Blue for date, stitches under alphabet and HOME SWEET HOME

A600   Dark green for leaves and stem on border

A611   Green for grass

D211   Dark red for house roof

A423   Brown for house roof

A430   Dark brown for edge of roof, front door frame and door knocker

A445   Cream for window panes

Whiskers

The cats' whiskers were added after the needlepoint was finished with black cotton thread. The eyes and noses are tiny black beads.

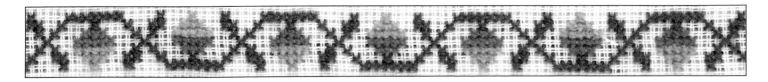

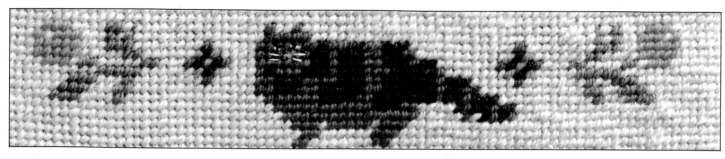

Stockists

An excellent shop providing a wide range of yarns, canvas and advice is:
CREATIVITY NEEDLECRAFTS
37/45 New Oxford Street
London WC1   Tel 071-240 2945

They also run a mail order service – send a SAE for lists to:
CREATIVITY NEEDLECRAFTS
15 Downing Street
Farnham
Surrey GU9 7PB

Also recommended:
THE PATCHWORK DOG & THE CALICO CAT
21 Chalk Farm Road
London NW1   Tel 071-485 1239
Open Tuesday to Sunday 10 – 6. Send SAE for catalogue.

I have found the John Lewis stores also well stocked.

Coats Leisure Craft Group who manufacture **Anchor Tapisserie** yarn tell me that it is widely stocked throughout the UK in the Craft Departments of most large department stores and Needlecraft shops. If you have any problems obtaining what you need write to:

DAVID MACLEOD
Marketing Manager
Coats Leisure Craft Group
39 Durham Street
Glasgow G41 1BS

USA Distributor
SUSAN BATES Inc
212 Middlesex Avenue
Chester
Connecticut 06412

DMC yarns are also widely available throughout the UK. In case of difficulty, write to:
DUNLICRAFT Ltd
Pullman Road
Wigston
Leicester LE8 2DY

enclosing an SAE for list of stockists.

For USA stockists, write to:
ROBERT KOREN
Vice President, Marketing
DMC Corporation
Port Kearny Buildings#10
South Kearny
NJ 07032 - 0650

Australia
MRS KARL PAPAS
DMC Needlecraft (Pty) Ltd
99–101 Lakemba Street
PO Box 131
Belmore 2192
New South Wales
Australia

Paterna Persian stockists, write to:

Paterna Persian
PO Box 13
Albion Mills
Wakefield
West Yorkshire WF2 9SG

USA
JOHNSON CREATIVE ARTS Inc
445 Main Street
West Townsend
MAO 1474

Thanks

Thank you to Julia Dummett who stitched Tiny Tom; Valerie Woodburn who stitched the Cross Stitch Cats; Deborah Winthrop who stitched the portrait of Linus and Henrietta Garside who stitched the small cat on this page. Raymond Turvey drew the stitch diagrams.